A Turkish Cookbook
For Beginners

Copyright
All Information in this book is copyright to C.K   dia Enterprises, L.L.C. and may not be copied from, ren   old without prior written permission.

Disclaimer
The information co   for general information and en   , and **does not constitute medical, ps   ..er professional advice on any subject matter.**   . this book **is not a doctor and make no claims to be o**   ..u does not accept any responsibility for any loss which may arise from reliance on information contained within this book or on any associated websites or blogs. The author of this book is NOT a licensed therapist and makes no claims to be. To read from here onward, it is assumed the reader has taken the diligence to read this message

A Turkish Cookbook for Beginners

Disclaimer 1
Introduction 4
   How to Cook 6
   Equipment 9
   Procuring Exotic Ingredients 9
STARTERS, APPETIZERS AND BASICS 11
   Baba Ghanoush 12
   Basic Borek 13
   Basic Börülce Side Dish 15
   Cacik 16
   Çoban Salata 17
   Etli Pırasa 18
   Homemade Yogurt 19
   Ispanak / Turkish Spinach Dish 20
   Kahvaltı Salatası 21
   Kısır 22
   Kofte - Turkish Meatballs 23
   Kuskus 24
   Menemen 25
   Mercimek Koftesi (Lentil Pates) 26
   Mercimek Yemeği 27
   Muhlama 27
   Pida (Turkish Flat Cake) 28
   Potato Börek 29
   Sarma 30
   Shakshouka 32

Simit Bread 33

Stuffed Baked Potato (Kumpir) 35

Yayla Corbasi...AKA Yogurt Soup 37

Zeytinyağlı Fasülye 38

Zucchini Mücver 39

MAIN DISHES 41

Ali Nazik 42

Basic Turkish Bulgur Lamb Dish 43

Etli Bakla 44

Etli Dolma 46

İmam Bayildi 48

Ispanak Kavurma 49

Karnıyarık (Turkish Split-Belly Eggplant) 50

Manti with Yogurt Sauce (AKA Turkish Ravioli!) 52

Potatoes and Eggs (Patatesli Yumurta) 54

White Beans Plaki 55

Yoğurtlu Şhish Kofte 56

DESSERT 58

Apricot Compote (Kayisi Kompostosu) 58

Baklava 59

İncir tatlı 61

Muhallebi 62

Semolina Halva 64

Introduction

To understand Turkish food, we must first try to understand Turkey itself. The Turkish Empire was otherwise known as the Ottoman Empire. They were responsible, according to some historians, for "ending" the medieval period the day that Constantinople (present day Istanbul) was besieged and taken from the Holy Roman Empire in 1453. This was the last breath of the Roman Empire itself, which as we know had existed in some form (whether as an Empire or a Republic) for almost 2,500 years up until then. The Holy Roman Empire was established in the new grand churches of Constantinople in the 300s after Constantine the Great broke from the Western half of the empire and established the new Christian powered nation. Centuries later, for the Ottomans to sack Constantinople and convert the ancient churches into mosques spelt the doom of Constantine's vision, and it created a threat to the power structures of medieval Europe.

However, the new Istanbul would not be a closed off society built on strict religious grounds. Influence from Middle Eastern kingdoms during that time did not spell cultural collapse, but usually the opposite, as historically the old Islamic empires were known for preservation of antiquities and a push toward topics like science, mathematics, and education. Although initially Constantinople was a ransacked, broken city, it would gradually turn into a new cultural center, where even former enemies (Christians) were allowed to re-enter and live among Muslims (although they were taxed for their faith).

As all things must run their course, just like the Holy Roman Empire before it, the Ottoman Empire too crumbled. The Ottomans decided to join the Central Powers during the Great War (WWI), motivated perhaps by a self-interest to seize more power and territory. This, however, spelt the doom of the Empire. At the end of the war, Europe was a wreck, the Ottomans surrendered to the Allied powers, and the German and Austro-Hungarian empires were no more. Unfavorable terms of surrender led to the total dissolution of the Ottoman Empire as well, and it was officially non-existent by 1923, effectively ending the age of empires that had maintained for thousands of years. In its place would be a new Republic known as Turkey, which still encapsulated a very large portion of former Ottoman territory.

In Turkey there is a clear combination of Greek / Roman / Mediterranean and Middle Eastern cuisine, and this is because of the cultural mesh between the East and the West that occurred as a result of the inclusive nature of the Ottomans. This is why, for instance, baklava is an evolution of Roman cakes known as placenta. Roman desserts were gradually influenced by Middle Eastern cuisine, creating a surprising blend of pasta (the Roman pastry base) with common Middle Eastern spices like cinnamon and mint. The influence goes both ways, as many famously "Greek" dishes are actually Turkish in origin.

Turkish cooking is the result of centuries of chefs experimenting with flavors across the entire massive expanse of the Ottoman Empire, working with local ingredients across Ottoman territories from Algeria and Egypt all the way to the Caucasus and Central Europe. For instance, the concept of the "kebab" which is a mainstay of Turkish food is of Persian origin, while the Byzantine influence introduced many common herbs in Turkish cooking like parsley.

A wise eater may also notice a surprisingly Chinese and Mongolian style to Turkish cooking. This is noticeable the first time one eats cubes of marinated beef or lamb on a bed of rice at a Turkish café. Mutton, dairy (inc. yogurt), root vegetables, harvested grains, rice and other hearty components were what the Turkish ancestors of Central Asia survived on, in similar ways to their Mongolian and Chinese counterparts a little further east. These nomadic, tribally influenced staples represent the heart and core of Turkish food.

Turkish cooking is typically bold and without hidden flavors. It does not possess subtle dimensions of flavor as one may find in, say, French cuisine. The purpose of a Turkish flavor is to experience just that flavor, along with a hearty and nutritiously balanced meal designed to keep what was once an Empire well-fed and satisfied. It's no surprise there are generous portions of staples like beef, lamb and potatoes, and the food is very utilitarian without many presentational aspects. That being said, the ages of cultural heritage also means the bold flavors are unique and very diverse, with strong combinations like mint and lamb or yogurt and garlic. As a result, Turkish food is much adored, and going out for Turkish food in the West—an activity also highlighted by sipping Turkish tea and smoking Turkish hookah—has become as common-place as going out for Chinese, Thai, or French.

How to Cook

As the title of the book suggests, I want anybody to be able to get good at cooking, so to do this I will now try to condense a bunch of wisdom in the next few pages.

How does somebody get started right away in a culinary practice? Well, in my opinion, there's no better place to start than with Turkish food.

The reason is because, as I just mentioned, Turkish cooking does not have to be extremely precise. If you add too much mint, or put too much garlic in your yogurt sauce—you're more likely to develop a better flavor than you are to ruin the dish. That's because of Turkish cuisines bold versus subtle distinctions. On the other hand, French or even Italian cooking is much easier to mess up.

I am often surprised how "newbies" at cooking become so intimidated by the practice. I've met some people who are scared to pick up a spatula even once. Sometimes I am told "All I can cook is top ramen!". Well, I have good news—if you can cook top ramen, you can handle some pretty challenging dishes. The reason is because cooking dehydrated ramen noodles involves many of the basics: boiling water, mixing ingredients, and paying close attention to what you're making. Ramen is actually challenging, because if you allow it to boil even a minute or two longer than it's supposed to, the ramen comes out mushy and tastes gross.

If you want to be a good cook, here are my pointers:

- **A Clean Kitchen Space**

Your kitchen does not have to be really large, but it should be clean and clear. There are two things to keep in mind: don't try to work around junk all over the counter, and don't let dirtiness accumulate while you cook. You should try to cook one step at a time. If you leave the bag of flour open on the counter after you're done using it, you're likely to knock it over later, or it could distract you from what you're doing.

- **Relax About Advanced Techniques**

People go to culinary school to learn some special skills. You might see a chef flipping all of the vegetables he or she is sautéing into the air repeatedly. This is a good technique, but you don't have to be able to do this. Just use a spatula and flip everything by hand. You may also see an advanced chef dicing a carrot like a machine into perfectly arranged and evenly cut slices. You have to know this if you are working in a fine dining restaurant creating award winning presentations, but for Turkish dishes for friends and family it's totally unnecessary. In fact the best Turkish food in the world can be found at cafes throughout Istanbul and those cooks don't care about presentation—sometimes it just looks like bowls of slop.

- **Understand What Brings Out Flavors**

There's a reason why fresh Brussels sprouts taste much more delicious when you bake them instead of boil them. That's because the juices soak together and enhance the rest of the dish, while the baking also caramelizes them (bringing out the sugar) which would be unnoticeable from a simple boil. Slow cooker recipes can also taste amazing for this same reason. This is also why a lot of Turkish cooking requires use of the oven.

- **Understand What Flavors You Can and Cannot Mix**

Recipes are good because they lay everything out for you, but to be adventurous you have to be careful. When you bake two or more items together, those recipes will bleed into each other. If you bake some Brussels sprouts with some carrots, I think it's safe to say you'll have a good tasting vegetable dish. If you bake Brussels sprouts with tomatoes I'd be worried about the acidic tomatoes overriding the Brussels sprout's flavor, or the tomato juice making them soggy. If you bake Brussels sprouts with something weird like ketchup, you're asking for trouble as these are flavors that do not blend together. Just because one item tastes good by itself does NOT mean it will taste good with a second item that also tastes good by itself.

Furthermore, never underestimate the power of a single item's flavor. You don't need to go overboard with most dishes. 9 times out of 10 simplicity is better than complication. For instance, if you are roasting some lamb, the lamb's own juices will enhance it's flavor better than anything else you can put in the dish.

Finally, don't overwhelm a dish with two matching elements. An example would be: if a dish is already hot, don't add hot mustard to it because you won't even be able to notice it underneath its existing heat structure. **If you're ever in doubt, ask the Google God "Can I mix ingredient X and ingredient Y?"**

- **Taste Test Sensitive to Cook Food Repeatedly**

The main reason people overcook or undercook pasta is because they don't taste test it. Boil it for the suggested time, then take out a noodle or a bit of rice and determine if it's al-dente or really just undercooked. Boil another 3-4 minutes, taste test again, then use your best judgment and turn the skillet off.

- **Some Ingredients Must be Measured**

You don't have to obsessively measure out one flat teaspoon of parsley (I'd just throw in a couple pinches) but for something sensitive to the whole dish, for instance baking soda, you should be precise. The same can be said for large amounts of any ingredient. If a dish requires 300 ML of milk, trying to eyeball this is very hard and you could end up with too much, turning everything into a soup.

- **Pay Attention!**

Finally, do not go wandering off while something cooks, unless it's a long baking procedure. You need to stay on top of what you're making and try to focus on it as best as you can.

Equipment

You will find anything you need at any department store. You can get by with one medium size pot, 1-2 smaller mixing bowls, one medium size skillet (I prefer stone ground skillets that reduce sticking), 1-2 medium to large size casserole / baking dishes, one medium size sharp knife, a ladle, a spatula, a food processor, an oven, and a few measuring cups. An egg timer is useful, as well. Finally, you do need a few Tupperware containers to store leftovers.

Procuring Exotic Ingredients

For this cookbook, the fresher and more regional the ingredients, the better. In Turkey, people may buy their supplies from the famous night bazaars, where vendors have sold bags of spices, grains and other ingredients for centuries. If you live somewhere like the USA, you may not have anything like this anywhere you live. However, you can still go to farmer's markets which are a decent alternative. I also find organic chains like Whole Foods to have better, fresher selections of spices than regular grocery stores. Finally, for something you're having trouble locating, find an ethnic import grocery store, and it's sure to have what you're looking for it.

STARTERS, APPETIZERS AND BASICS

In Turkish cuisine, an appetizer may not always be an appetizer. A portion of sarmas, some yogurt soup, a few fritters—these can all be put together for a great meal. Smaller dishes may be combined together for an impressive array. As a result, you will find more of these lighter meals in Turkish cooking than larger single courses.

Baba Ghanoush

No Turkish or Mediterranean dining experience is complete without a helping of this famous eggplant dish with a side of pita bread.

Ingredients

1 medium eggplant
2 garlic cloves, peeled
3 tablespoons tahini paste
4 tablespoons lemon juice
1/2 teaspoon salt
1 tablespoon minced Italian parsley
Olive oil

Preparation

The eggplant will be prepared in your oven's broiler. Preheat the broiler (350 F). Place a few small incisions into your eggplant, and place it on a foil-lined baking tray, underneath the broiler. When the skin chars on one side, turn the eggplant by a 1/4th turn. Continue until entire skin is charred and the pulp is soft and mushy. Peel away the skin, rinsing to remove all of the charred skin.

Next, in a blender or a food processor, add all of the remaining ingredients together until you create a fine paste. Create a small indentation in each serving with the back of a spoon, and add a tablespoon of olive oil; so that the oil sits on top (as in picture). Serve with pita bread.

Basic Borek

These flaky pastries are filled with delicious cheeses, but other recipes may call for meats like lamb to be added.

Ingredients
6 big yufka sheets (flatbread)
4 cups milk
4 eggs
125 grams butter or margarine
1 tea spoon of salt
½ tea spoon. black pepper or white pepper
18 ounces crumbled Turkish white cheese, reduced salt Feta, or crumbly goat cheese
4 table spoon. chopped Italian parsley

Prep Time: 15 minutes
Cook Time: 45 minutes

Preparation

Before we get started, first procure some yufka sheets. This is a Turkish flatbread that is simple to make. Homemade varieties will taste better than packaged ones.

In a large microwave safe bowl, add butter and melt it in the microwave or a separate pan. Mix milk, salt, pepper and microwave or pan cook until warm.

In a separate bowl, add the variety of cheeses and chopped parsley.

Butter the bottom and sides of a big, oven-proof baking tray. Drizzle a spoonful or two of the milk mixture over the bottom. Next, take the first sheet of yufka and place it in an uneven, wrinkly fashion to cover the bottom of the tray. Spoon about 1/6 of the milk mixture all over the yufka. Let it run into the cracks and crevices and around the edges.

Distribute the cheese mixture roughly into five parts. Sprinkle 1/5 of the cheese mixture over the yufka. Now, do the same with the next layer. Repeat after you have five layers finished. Cover the top of your pastry completely with the last piece of yufka. Drizzle the last portion of the milk mixture over the top, wetting all of it.

Sprinkle the top of your pastry with sesame seeds or black cumin. Bake it in a 185° F / 365° C oven for about 45 minutes, or until the top is nicely browned and the center is firm.

When your pastry is cooked, remove the pan from oven and sprinkle one or two tablespoons of cold water over the top, then wrap the whole thing in clean butcher's paper or a clean towel. This helps to soften the top layer. Let the pastry rest for about 20 minutes before cutting it into squares.

Basic Börülce Side Dish

Börülce is the Turkish name for what you may know as black eyed peas. Not just an overrated pop group, these legumes are actually a very healthy addition to your diet that can be found in numerous Turkish recipes.

Ingredients

1 cup black-eyed peas
50 ml extra virgin olive oil
2 table spoon tomato paste
1 cup hot water
1 table spoon sugar
1 tea spoon salt

Preparation

Boil the black-eyed peas in 3-4 cups of water for about 20 minutes until they are soft. Then wash and drain them. Add to a medium sized cooking pot with the rest of the ingredients and continue cooking for about 20-25 minutes on medium heat. You can add more salt, or more water to create soupier consistency, Serve with bread.

Cacik

This yogurt dish is strained or diluted to create a delicious, minty taste. It is a great palate cleanser to eat after a larger meal. Variations can be found throughout the Balkans and in Greece, as well.

Ingredients

2 cups plain yogurt
1 cup of cold water
½ tsp dried oregano
¼ cup fresh dill weed
3 medium cucumbers, peeled and diced very small
2 cloves garlic, diced very small
Salt
2 tablespoons ground and dried mint
2 tablespoons extra virgin olive oil

Preparation

Place yogurt in a big bowl. Add all of the ingredients, except salt and water, and mix thoroughly.

Add water until required consistency is achieved. Mix in some salt, taste and add more if required.

Chill in the refrigerator for about two hours before serving. Alternatively you can make this with a fine mesh strainer to remove the larger chunks of herbs / spices to keep the yogurt purer after the flavor is added.

Çoban Salata

Flavorful Turkish salads are known for two important ingredients: parsley and mint. Coban salata is known to also contain a variety of peppers, onion and feta cheese—similar to other Mediterranean salads.

Ingredients
1/2 cup cucumber, diced
2 tomatoes, diced
1 cubanelle pepper, chopped
½ cup flat-leaf parsley, chopped
1/4 red onion, sliced
1/4 cup fresh mint, chopped

Dressing:
2-3 table spoon extra virgin olive oil
2 tbsp vinegar
½ cup feta cheese, crumbled
Salt
Pepper

Preparation

Simply add the diced and sorted vegetables together, tossing into a large bowl. Add the dressing and cheese and enjoy.

Etli Pırasa

A bit like a stew. This dish can be found in the windows of cafes throughout Istanbul.

Ingredients

1 bunch of leeks (3 sticks), cut in chunks, washed several times
1 small carrot, peeled, sliced
4-5 sliced baby onions

1 stalk sliced celery
1 cup gr lamb, cut in cubes
1 table spoon butter
1 table spoon extra virgin olive oil
1 table spoon flour
1 + 1 1/4 cup hot water
Salt
Pepper

Sauce:
1 egg yolk
4 table spoon lemon juice

Preparation

Cook the lamb cubes in their own juice at medium-low heat. Then add 1 cup of hot water, cook at medium-low heat until most of the water evaporates and the lamb pieces soften. Add the leek, carrot, sliced onion, celery, butter, olive oil, 1 1/4 cup hot water, salt and pepper. Sprinkle the flour all over and mix.

Cover the lid halfway and cook for about 20 minutes over medium heat. In a small bowl, whisk the egg yolk with lemon juice. Take a few spoon of juice of the dish and blend well with the sauce. Slowly pour this mixture into the pot while mixing. Cover the lid and simmer for about 3-4 minutes. Serve it while hot with bread or pita.

3 servings.

Homemade Yogurt

For most of the dishes outlined in this book that use yogurt, I suggest to make your yogurt from scratch, preferably using fresh ingredients from a farmer's market. Commerical yogurt is never quite as good.

Ingredients

4 cups milk

2 cups half-and-half
3 -4 tablespoons cultured yogurt

Preparation

Put the milk and cream into a cooking pot on medium until it is very hot but not boiling. If you boil it, the milk can burn and ruin it. When it's just hot enough, turn off the heat and let it cool until it's medium-hot, then add 3-4 tablespoons of your cultured yogurt. Allow it to sit.

When the milk has cooled down more, add some to the cup with the yogurt. Next mix well and then add back into the pot of milk, mix again. Next take a clean glass jar or an ovenproof bowl and pour the milk into it, mix well. Cover the jar/bowl with plastic wrap and then a dish cloth.

Now the fun part: take a desk lamp with about a 75 watt bulb, hook it up in your kitchen and then point it toward the surface of the jar/bowl (about 6 inches away). Let the jar/bowl with the milk and yogurt starter incubate under the heat lamp for about 8 to 12 hours. I prefer 12 hours. The finished yogurt should be tangy.

Ispanak / Turkish Spinach Dish

This can be served by itself or as a filling for various Turkish pastry dishes.

Ingredients

750 g fresh spinach or 1 (250 g) package frozen spinach, chopped
1 onion, finely chopped
2 tablespoons olive oil
1/2 cup feta cheese, crumbled (beyaz peynir)
1 egg, beaten
1/4 cup parsley, finely chopped
salt & freshly ground black pepper

Preparation

Prepare fresh spinach by washing it and removing brown and dead bits. Chop on wooden cutting board until it becomes well-diced. Place in large pan, cover, and steam over medium heat for 7-8 minutes or until wilted. Place fresh wilted or defrosted frozen spinach in a sieve and press with the back of a spoon to extract moisture. Transfer to a bowl. Now, saute the onion in the oil until transparent and add this to the spinach with cheese, egg and parsley.

Combine ingredients thoroughly, seasoning to taste with salt and pepper.

Kahvaltı Salatası

Another great salad that is often served in a way that looks very presentational, with cucumber, cherry tomatoes and egg as the featured parts of it.

Ingredients
Cherry tomatoes, cut in half
Cucumber, cut into bite size slices.
Red onion, sliced
Feta cheese
Egg, hard boiled, sliced or whole (placed in center)
Sprinkled oregano
Salt
Pepper
Optional: Thin sliced ham or other meats

Dressing:
Lemon juice + Extra virgin olive oil

Preparation

Instead of tossing, arrange carefully on a dinner platter and serve. Enjoy at any time of day.

Kısır

Traditionally a side dish. Made with bulgur wheat as the primary ingredient.

Ingredients

1 cup **bulgur wheat**, big grain
60 ml olive oil
1 onion, diced
1-2 table spoon tomato paste
1 lemon juice
1/2 tea spoon salt
1 table spoon cumin

Preparation

In a large bowl, empty your bag of bulgur wheat and pour two cups of water into it, and allow it to soak for about five minutes. Meanwhile in a medium sized pot, place the onion and olive oil.

Cook until the onions turn light brown. Add the salt, tomato paste, lemon juice and cumin.

Then wash and drain the bulgur, and mix it into the pot with a wooden spoon. Cook for about 10 minutes on medium-low heat. Afterwards, cover and set aside for it to cool down.

When it's cold, add in the following:

3-4 tomatoes, diced
4-5 fresh green onions, diced
1 cup chopped parsley

Keep refrigerated as Kisir is best served cold.

Kofte - Turkish Meatballs

Kofte can be turned into wraps, pita sandwiches, or served by themselves as a main course. Unlike western meatballs, kofte is more fragant with herbs and spices. You are less likely to find kofte with pasta as with Italian spaighetti and meatballs. You cannot walk one yard in any Turkish city without finding some type of kofte vendor.

Ingredients

1 1/2 pound lean ground lamb (or beef)
1 medium onion, grated
1 cup white breadcrumb
1 tablespoon water
2 eggs
1/4 cup fresh parsley, finely chopped
1/4 cup of fresh mint, finely chopped (or 1 1/2 tablespoons of dried mint)
1/2 teaspoon salt (or to taste)
1/2 teaspoon white pepper

Preparation

Use a medium mixing bowl and mx all of the ingredients together, kneading together with your hands (wash your hands after). Next you want the flavors to be soaked up by the ground lamb, so leave in the fridge for several hours. When they're ready, begin rolling into even golf-ball sized balls with your hands.

Add a little olive oil on a cookie sheet covered with foil and bake for 35 to 45 minutes at 350 degrees or until Kofte is cooked through. Serve with pita bread, Cacik, salad or regular yogurt.

Kuskus

This is a staple dish all over the Middle East and many parts of Africa. Knowing how to make kuskus (or couscous) creates possibilities for many other types of recipes, as well.

Ingredients
1 cup dry couscous… Available at the pasta aisle at almost any grocer.
2 1/2 cup hot chicken broth

2 table spoon butter
Salt

Preparation

Saute the pasta with the butter for a few minutes in a pot. Add the hot chicken broth and salt, cover the lid halfway and boil for about 15 minutes over medium-low heat. Turn the heat off and put aside for 20 minutes. Mix with a fork and serve.

For quick Turkish cooking, just make some couscous with a side of roasted lamb cutlet, chicken, and / or yogurt.

Menemen

This is a Turkish style "scrambled eggs" dish that you'll find commonly served in cafes throughout Turkey as a light meal, suitable for any time of the day or as an appetizer for a larger course.

Ingredients

1 big onion finely chopped
3 tomatoes petite diced
1 fresh green pepper diced
3-4 whole eggs
2 table spoon olive oil
Salt
Pepper

Preparation

1: Saute chopped onions with oil in a medium skillet. Add green pepper, saute more until tender. Add diced tomatoes and mix to combine.

2. Sprinkle some salt and pepper to taste. When tomatoes become soft, crack the eggs. You can mix them well or you may leave the eggs on top without mixing until cooked.

Mercimek Koftesi (Lentil Pates)

Bulgur, or Turkish wheat, can be made into these lightly filling pates.

Ingredients

½ cup red lentil, washed and drained
1 cup fine bulgur
2 ½ cups water
1 onion, chopped finely
2 table spoon tomato paste
¼ cup olive oil
½ tea spoon black pepper
1/3 tea spoon cumin
1 tea spoon salt to taste
¼ cup hot water
½ bunch fresh parsley, chopped finely
½ tea spoon dried mint/3-4 pairs of fresh mint, chopped finely
2 green onions, only green parts chopped finely
Lettuce leaves or arugula
Lemon wedges

Preparation

Boil red lentil with 2 ½ cup of water until lentils are soft but there is still some water in the bottom. Turn the heat off and mix in fine bulgur, close the lid. Leave for at least 10 minutes to make the bulgur absorb all the water and expand.

Meanwhile, sauté onions with olive oil over medium heat. And then mix in tomato paste. Saute for 1-2 minutes and add salt and hot water. Transfer to the pot with bulgur and red lentils. Mix in spices, green onions and parsley. Mix them all. If the mixture sticks, wet your hands with water occasionally.

Serve Lentil Pates with lettuce leaves or arugula and lemon wedges. Also keep them in the fridge.

Mercimek Yemeği

This is a Turkish lentil soup with a hearty supply of lentils.

Ingredients

3/4 cup lentils, soak in water overnight, washed and drained
1 onion, finely chopped
50 ml extra virgin olive oil
1 tea spoon cumin
3 table spoon crushed tomatoes, canned
1 table spoon orzo, optional
2 cups warm chicken stock or beef stock or just water

Preparation

First cook the onion in the olive oil in a cooking pot for about 3-4 minutes. Add the lentils and saute for another 4-5 minutes. Add the rest of the ingredients and stir with a wooden spatula. Cover and cook for about 20-25 minutes at medium-low heat until the lentils are soft. Mix, serve..

Makes 2-3 servings.

Muhlama

A light corn-flour "pasta" appetizer. To get the best result with home cooked muhlama, experts suggest to find ingredients from the Black Sea region, if possible as they say the local cheeses, butter, and cream from this region has a special flavor.

Ingredients

Ingredients:
1 cup of corn flour

½ cup butter
2/3rd cup of Telli Muhlama cheese, if you can find it. You may also use feta.
1 glass of water

Preparation

Melt butter on low heat, add corn flour and mix for a while, as the flour turns pinkish, add the hot water gradually, and keep mixing until the mixture starts to form into the consistency of a pasta. Then, you should blend the cheese with a wooden ladle or spoon and mix until evenly blended. Can be served any time of the day.

Pida (Turkish Flat Cake)

This is the staple food around Turkey and much of the Middle East. You'll find it served with many other dishes and it's good to know how to keep a supply on hand.

Ingredients

4 cups of flour
1 ½ tbsp. yeast
½ cup of water
1 teaspoon olive oil
1 teaspoon sesame seeds
1 teaspoon black sesame seed
1 teaspoon salt

Preparation

Stir the yeast and water together in a wooden mixing bowl, then add the flour and knead with salt into a dough.

After the dough is finished, cover it with a wet towel and leave in a warm place for 30 minutes to rise. Use a knife or slicer to cut the dough into 2 pieces, and form these into two round cakes.

Brush these dough balls with olive oil and sprinkle sesame seeds over it, and then bake at 180 C / 350 F for 20 minutes.

Potato Börek

Borek dishes are traditionally flaky pastries filled with meats, vegetables and other ingredients. However, it's also possible to make borek out of potatoes. This recipe is similar to a kind of shepherd's pie.

Ingredients

1 cup vegetable oil
1 cup yogurt
2 eggs
4 medium sized potatoes, mashed
3 onions, chopped
1 carrot, peeled, cut in cubes
1/2 cup sweet peas, frozen, soaked in hot water and drained
1 tea spoon mint
1 tea spoon cumin
1 tea spoon cayenne pepper
1 tea spoon salt
½ cup ground lamb (optional)

13x9x2 oven dish

Preparation

Microwave or bake the potatoes until soft. Afterward, lightly mash them. For additional flavor, add a tablespoon of butter to the potatoes.

Whisk the vegetable oil, eggs and yogurt in a bowl. Add the rest of the ingredients except for the potatoes, and mix. Slowly add the flour in and knead everything together. Spread equally into the oven dish. Add the potatoes as an even layer across the top.

Preheat the oven to 400 F. Bake for about 40-45 minutes.

Sarma

Sarma is maybe the ubiquitous Turkish dish. It is found all across the region. It consists generally of stuffed grape leaves. At your local Turkish restaurant you may find Sarma as an appetizer. In some places, it could be the main course. The ingredients may also change from region to region.

Ingredients

50-60 fresh or preserved grape leaves (+ a few extra for the bottom of the pan)
1 of cup rice
2 small tomatoes
1 medium onion
2 cloves of garlic
A handful of parsley
A handful of dill
3/4 cup of water

1/2 table spoon of dried mint or a few fresh mint leaves
1/4 cup of olive oil
Lemon juice of 1/2 lemon or a few slices lemon to put on top while cooking
1 table spoon of salca (Turkish mixture of paprika/tomato or pure tomato paste, sundried)
1 teaspoon of ground cumin
1 teaspoon of ground pepper
1 teaspoon salt - if you are using salty preserved grape leaves, then skip adding extra salt as the salca is already salty enough

Preparation

You may be able to find salca or a very similar Balkan equivalent at your local ethnic grocery store. Otherwise, you can make it yourself with some fresh ground paprika.

Chop the onion, tomatoes, parsley, dill and garlic finely. Set a cooking or frying pan on medium heat and in it combine the rice, salca, chopped tomatoes, onion and the water. Mix for two or three minutes until the salca is mostly dissolved. Add the lemon juice, olive oil, parsley, dill, dried or fresh mint and the spices. Continue mixing for another 2-3 minutes. You don't want your rice to be cooked thoroughly, the real cooking will come later. This is just a little startup.

Set your rice mixture aside to cool before you continue with the stuffing process. Meanwhile start rinsing your grape leaves. Sometimes preserved grape leaves are very salty, so in this case— rinse them well.

Now we need to actually arrange the sarmas into the cooking pan. To prevent the sarmas from sticking to the bottom of the pan, you should first cover the bottom with the few extra grape leaves. Once you begin to place them, it's important that you make sure that there isn't too much space left between them. You should use a porcelain plate or cooking dish and put it upside down on top of the sarmas. This will help the sarmas keep their shape.

Add water to the cooking pan (if you are using a plate, do this before you add the water), the water should cover the sarmas, but should only barely touch the sides of your disk or your plate.

Put the cooking pan on medium-high heat until the water starts heating. When the water begins to boil lightly, turn your heat to low and let it simmer for about 30-40 minutes. You can cook less for al-dente variety, but it's better softer. Just be careful not to overcook, it's easy to cook rice too long and ruin the dish, which means for these types of recipes you should frequently perform taste tests.

Serve your sarma with Turkish yogurt, the Cacik recipe from elsewhere in this book, and / or some paprika powder sprinkled on top of it!

Shakshouka

Poached eggs in a basic sauce of tomatoes. This recipe is very simple and could be served for breakfast, dinner, or as a side.

<u>Ingredients</u>

1 big onion (finely chopped)
4 eggs
Cooking oil as needed
6 medium tomatoes
Salt and pepper

Preparation

In a big frying pan, saute onion until lightly browned. Grate the tomatoes on largest holes of a grater. Mix grated tomatoes and onion, cover and cook over low heat for 25 minutes Remove cover and break eggs over the surface. Mix gently to break yolks, cover and cook for about 3 or 4 minutes until eggs are set. Sprinkle with salt and pepper.

Simit Bread

These are known as Turkish sesame bread rings. A well-made Simit bread has a spiraling shape, is lightly sweet, and can be turned into a sweeter dish with the addition of a spice like cinnamon. What you will find is that many regions from Macedonia through Greece and specific cities like Ezmir and Istanbul have different types of Simit, with different consistencies, levels of sweetness, and shapes.

Ingredients

White bread flour, 3.5 cups
Water, 400 ml
Yeast, 2 teaspoons
Honey, about 1 table spoon
Sesame seeds, about 1 cup
Olive oil, about 2 table spoons

Preparation

Mix water, yeast, olive oil and flour in bowl. Knead well. Cover the bowl and leave at room temperature for 30 minutes to an hour until it rises.

Now, take two little bowls, one for the water and one for the seeds.

Mix the honey with a cup of water. Make rings and dip the rings in the honeywater and then followed by dipping into the sesame seeds. Bake the bread at around 400 F in a pre-heated oven for 8-10 minutes.

Stuffed Baked Potato (Kumpir)

Everybody is familiar with stuffed, baked potatoes. The Turkish name for such a dish is kumpir. The recipe may vary quite a bit from the West. It is common street food but may also be found in fine dining restaurants.

Ingredients

1 big sweet or yellow potato
1 table spoon butter
2-3 table spoon mozzarella/ cheddar /parmesan, shredded
A pinch of salt

Filling options:
Grated carrots
Sliced pickles
Green olives /pepper stuffed green olives, sliced

Black olives, sliced
Ground lamb
Sweet corn
Coleslaw
Sweet peas
Red cabbage, sliced finely (squeezed with salt, washed and drained)
Chopped dill
Ketchup
Horseradish Mustard
Sour Cream

Preparation

You can prepare a stuffed potato in the microwave or in the oven, but either case be sure to pierce the potato several times first. For the oven, preheat to 425 F (220 C) until the potato is soft. For the microwave, 10-15 minutes will do the trick. Then, it is simply a matter of cutting the potato lengthwise and adding the ingredients. You may want to cut another slit in the center of each potato help hold the ingredients together. Olives, ground lamb, dill, and other herbs (even mint) creates are more authentically Turkish stuffed potato.

Yayla Corbasi…AKA Yogurt Soup

Made with a variety of herbs, rice, flour, and yogurt—this is a much loved Turkish utilization of yogurt in a way that few other dishes ever incorporate it.

<u>Ingredients</u>
6 cups of water
1 block of bullion
1/2 cup white rice
2 cups of Greek yogurt
1/2 cup milk
1 egg white separated
1/2 cup flour,
For flavour
2 table spoon butter
1 table spoon dry mint
1 tsp dried tarragon
Salt

Preparation

Boil the water, rice, salt and bullion. Cook at medium-high, until the rice is done.

Meanwhile in a bowl, mix yogurt, milk, egg yolk and flour. After the rice is cooked, take a few spoons of liquid from the pot and mix into the bowl. Then slowly pour your mixture into the pot while mixing very slowly. Cook for 10 more minutes at low heat.

Place the butter in a pan. When it begins boiling, mix in the mint and pour into your soup.

Serve immediately. Makes 4 servings.

Zeytinyağlı Fasülye

A recipe for vegetable lovers.

Ingredients

2 ½ cups of flat beans, wash, cut both ends
½ cup extra virgin olive oil (half for cooking, half for after cooking)
1 small onion, chopped
1 garlic clove, chopped
1 tablespoon sugar
2 tomatoes, peeled, diced
1 table spoon canned crushed tomatoes
1 1/2 cups warm water
Salt

Preparation

In a medium size pot with a lid; saute the onion in the olive oil for 3-4 minutes. Then, add beans, tomatoes, crushed tomatoes, garlic, sugar and salt. Add 1 cup of water, and leave the lid half open to release steam. Simmer for 35-40 minutes until everything is tender, and add another half cup of water halfway through.

Let it cool down in the pot. Then, serve. Makes about 3 servings.

Zucchini Mücver

Turkish fritters can come in a variety of styles, from savory, meaty, to sweet. This recipe calls for an assortment of herbs plus feta cheese and zucchini, and makes an excellent lunch.

Ingredients
1 medium zucchini
1/2 cup feta cheese
2-3 green onions, chopped
1/2 cup parsley, chopped
1/2 cup fresh dill, chopped
1 table spoon flour
2-3 garlic cloves, chopped
1 2 eggs
1 tea spoon baking powder
Black pepper
Preparation

Mesh the zucchini into thin pieces and squeeze with your hands to drain water out. Add all the ingredients above, with the egg, and knead together in a bowl. In a medium skillet, add the vegetable oil, and then take a lump of the mixture and put it in the skillet. Fry each side approximately 3 minutes at medium-high heat. At last, put the pieces on a plate with a paper towel to dry the oil. Serve with our familiar yogurt garlic sauce.

MAIN DISHES

While the dishes found in common cafes are often smaller portioned meals divided up in a way that you can pick and choose, for nighttime dining in restaurants you will still be presented with the "main course" which usually features richer, rarer ingredients and much fancier presentations. Here are some of the most well recognized main dishes.

Ali Nazik

From the Gaziantep province of Turkey comes this delicious main course that combines many Turkish specialties like peppers, eggplant, lamb and yogurt.

Ingredients

2 medium eggplants
2 large bell peppers
150 gr ground lamb or beef, cooked with salt and pepper
1/2 cup Turkish yogurt sauce (mix yogurt with 1 clove of crushed garlic mixed with salt)

Garnish:
1 table spoon butter
1 tea spoon red pepper, powdered
1/2 tea spoon Cayenne pepper, powdered

Preparation

Prepare eggplants by slicing holes in them to help them cook. Set oven to broil, and prepare eggplants and pepper on an oven tray. Begin the roast. Remove the green pepper after about 20 minutes and then remove the eggplant 5-10 minutes later. Turn both over occasionally during cooking.

Peel off the skins from both the eggplant and green pepper (discard seeds), and cut in small pieces. Put them in a glass Pyrex dish. Turn off the oven, and return to the inside of the oven to keep warm.

When the rest of the ingredients are prepared, take the Pyrex out of the oven and pour the yogurt on top to create a bed of yogurt. Then put the cooked ground beef or lamb directly on top of the yogurt.

Finally, melt the butter in a small pan and add the peppers. When it starts bubbling, pour over the ground beef. You can serve with pita bread and / or sliced tomato on the sides of plate.

Serve Ali Nazik immediately while still warm.

Basic Turkish Bulgur Lamb Dish

Bulgur is a dry, cracked wheat made from several different species of wheat. There are various ways to prepare the dish after you've purchased a bag of bulgur. Here is one.

Ingredients
400g (14oz) lamb cubes
3/4 cup Turkish bulgur, big-grain, washed, drained
4 table spoon extra virgin olive oil
2 small onion, sliced
2 long red pepper, discard the seeds, chopped
2 garlic clove, chopped
3 table spoon tomato sauce
2 tea spoon red pepper sauce
Salt
Pepper

Garnish:
Dry mint
Red pepper flakes

Preparation

In a medium sized post, add some water and the lamb cubes

Prepare lamb cubes with a few tbsp of water in a medium-size cooking pot. Cook the lamb cubes at medium heat until there is no water left. Add the butter, olive oil, onion, and peppers. Continue to sauté for 2-3 more minutes. Then add the garlic, tomato paste and red pepper paste. While mixing, sauté for about one minute. Add the bulgur and hot beef broth and then continue to mix.

Turn the heat down to low. Cover and cook until all the water evaporates. Let the Pilav stand for about 5 minutes. Garnish with dry mint and red pepper flakes. Makes 4 servings.

Etli Bakla

This main course features fava beans with lamb and more use of the commonly implemented garlic yogurt sauce.

Ingredients

2 cups of fava beans, washed, cut both ends and shave along the sides with a knife.
1 cup ground lamb, cut in cubes
1 medium size onion, chopped
4-5 tablespoon extra virgin olive oil
1 spoon full red pepper paste
1 table spoon butter
1 + 1 1/2 cup hot water
Salt

Garlic Yogurt Sauce (same as other instances in this book):
1/2 cup Turkish yogurt
1 garlic clove, mashed with 1/2 tea spoon salt
Optional: 2 table spoon dill, chopped

Preparation

Cook the lamb cubes in their own juices. After all the water evaporates, add the onion, butter and olive oil, and then saute for a few minutes. Add 1 cup of hot water, cook over medium-low heat until all the water evaporates and the lamb pieces are softened.

Then, add the red pepper paste and the fava beans. Saute over low heat until the bean's color turns to a yellowish hue. Mix occasionally. Then add 1 1/2 cup hot water and salt. Cover the lid halfway and cook for about 25-30 minutes at low medium heat. If necessary add more hot water.

Serve the final dish with the yogurt drizzled on top.

2-3 servings.

Etli Dolma

These are Turkish stuffed peppers.

Ingredients

6 bell peppers (small sized)
3 table spoon extra virgin olive oil
1 table spoon butter
1/2 cup canned crushed tomatoes
3/4 cup water

Stuffing Ingredients:
300 g medium ground beef
1 medium tomato, peeled, diced
1/2 cup rice, rinsed
1/2 cup Turkish bulgur, small grain, rinsed

4 fresh onions, chopped
1/3 cup parsley, chopped
2 table spoon dill, chopped
3 table spoon extra virgin olive oil
3 table spoon water
1 tea spoon paprika
Salt
Pepper

Garlic Yogurt Sauce:
1/2 cup plain yogurt
1 garlic clove, mashed with salt

Preparation

First cut off the tops of the peppers. You can discard the tops or use them to place back over the peppers later after the filling is added. Clean out the seeds from the inside of the peppers.

Mix together the filling ingredients in a bowl, and using a spoon carefully fill the peppers. Be careful not to overstuff them. Try to separate out even portions of the ingredients first.

Place into a large casserole dish and add the rest of the ingredients (crushed tomatoes, water, butter and olive oil). Bake at about 375 F for 45 minutes. Serve with the garlic yogurt sauce created separately. Serves 2-3.

İmam Bayildi

This is a stuffed eggplant dish. It uses a hearty portion of olive oil. The legend was the Imam who first cooked this dish made his wife faint when she found out that he went through their entire olive oil supply just to cook a few eggplants.

Ingredients
4 ripe eggplants
1 cup of olive oil
Salt
Lemon juice
4 garlic cloves, chopped
1 big onion (or 2 medium) cut in thin slices.
2 big tomatoes, skinned, deseeded and chopped
1/2 cup of chopped parsley

Preparation

First cut the ends off your eggplant and begin peeling the skin. For best presentational purposes, peel long strips off while leaving even gaps in-between (so you are leaving some skin on).

Begin to fry the eggplant in the oil until it appears golden colored. You may also decide to bake the eggplant at 345 F. After it's done cooking, put them aside.

Add some more oil to the pan and now fry / saute the onion, caramelizing it slightly (it should stay white in color). Add spices (the chopped garlic, parsley). Continue cooking with the spices, and halfway through add tomatoes, the paprika, pepper, salt. It will now be simmering. Add lemon juice and a pinch of sugar. Cook another 2-3 minutes.

Create a pocket in each eggplant using two forks, a spoon or your finger. You will need to split the eggplants from top to tail to make a boat like shape, but aim to avoid breaking all the way through.

Spoon the onion filling into the eggplant pockets and sprinkle the tops with remaining pan juices and olive oil. Now bake the whole dish 345 F for about 20 minutes.

Serve hot, or at room temperature.

Ispanak Kavurma

A popular spinach course that may conclude a series of lighter appetizers without over-filling the eater.

Ingredients
1 bunch spinach, washed and drained
2 table spoon rice, washed and drained
1 garlic clove, sliced
1 medium onion, sliced
1 medium tomato, diced
50 ml extra virgin olive oil
1 pinch red pepper
Salt
Pepper

Sauce:
1/2 cup yogurt
1 garlic clove, mashed with salt

Preparation

First cut the spinach in big pieces. In a medium pot, saute the onion in olive oil and then add the garlic. Cook for a few minutes until caramelized. Be careful not to burn the garlic. Then add the spinach, tomato, rice, red pepper, salt and black pepper in the pot. Cover the lid and cook for about 20 minutes (until the rice is cooked) on medium-low heat.

Serve Spinach with Rice with the yogurt sauce.

For a non-vegetarian alternative try adding ground lamb or beef.

Karnıyarık (Turkish Split-Belly Eggplant)

A common home-cooked eggplant dish found throughout Turkey.

Ingredients
4 medium long and skinny eggplant or several small ones

1 tablespoon of vegetable oil
200 g. lean ground beef
1 med. onion, finely chopped
4-6 cloves garlic, finely chopped
2 Tbsp. tomato paste diluted with ½ cup of water
1 Tbsp. cumin
1 Tbsp. Ottoman spice or paprika
1 ½ tea spoon. sugar
2 Tbsp salt and freshly ground black pepper
½ c. or a bit more of chopped parsley (I added a bit of chopped dill too.)
Garnish: sliced tomatoes and strips of sweet green peppers

Preparation

1: Preheat the oven to 400 F/200C.

2. First wash your eggplants and then peel them lengthwise with strips. Use a brush to cover each eggplant with vegetable oil. Make a slit down the middle of each one, but do not pierce it all the way through. This where you will be stuffing the meat filling later. Place the eggplant in a glass baking dish in a single layer.

3. Cook the eggplant until tender, about 15 to 20+ minutes, depending on the size of your eggplant. Rotate the eggplant while cooking so it cooks evenly.

4. While the eggplant is baking, make the filling. Just sauté the onion, adding garlic, in the vegetable oil until tender. Use a medium-size sauce pan for this.

5. Then add the ground beef and cook until browned, about 10 minutes. Add the tomato paste mixture, cumin, Ottoman spice or paprika, sugar, salt, freshly ground black pepper, parsley and dill. Continue mixing until most of the water is absorbed and remove from heat.

6. Slightly shape the eggplant with your fingers or a spoon to open the "bellies" so you can stuff them with the meat mixture. Place a tomato slice and two strips of green peppers (as seen in my photos) on top of the eggplant.

7. Pour the tomato sauce into baking dish around the eggplant. **For tomato sauce, whisk together 1 T. tomato paste and 1 T. pepper paste (or acı biber salçası) with 1 cup of hot water.

8. Continue roasting the eggplants for about 10-15 more minutes. You want to make sure the tomatoes and green peppers are properly roasted and tender. The green pepper should not be stiff.

9. Garnish the eggplant with a dollop of yogurt. Serve hot with rice pilav, salad, or flatbread.

Manti with Yogurt Sauce (AKA Turkish Ravioli!)

This is one of the most famous Turkish combinations. The lamb-stuffed pastas are similar to ravioli and are covered in two sauces: a garlic sauce made from yogurt, and a spicy one made from butter, paprika, and hot pepper, and the final presentation is garnished with mint. This dish, according to food historians, originated out of Mongolia, and ended up in the Ottoman court, spreading then amongst common folk in Anatolia. Even today, Manti remains the main dish in large dinner parties.

Ingredients

For the filling:
2 tablespoons olive oil
1 big onion, finely chopped
1 pound ground lean lamb
1/2 cup chopped fresh flat-leaf parsley
Salt and pepper to taste

For the pasta:
2 cups all-purpose flour, plus additional for rolling
1 teaspoon salt

1 big egg
1/2 cup water plus a little more if necessary

For the yogurt sauce:
2 cups plain whole-milk yogurt (experts suggest to use sheep's milk)
4 mashed garlic cloves with 1 tsp salt

For the butter sauce:
1/2 stick (1/4 cup) unsalted butter
3/4 teaspoon fine quality sweet paprika
Coarse salt to taste
4 dashes of hot red pepper sauce, or more to taste
Shredded fresh mint leaves for garnish

Preparation

First we should make the filling. Add olive oil to a large skillet and cook until it's hot, but make sure it doesn't start smoking (use low to moderate heat). Now saute the onion into the oil until it's soft, so about 5 minutes. You should then mix together the lamb and parsley, breaking up the lumps until the lamb changes from pink to a cooked color. Add a large amount of salt and pepper when this is finished, and set it aside.

To make the pasta: Add the flour and salt to a mixing bowl, and use your hands to create a well in the center, and then place the egg and 1/2 cup water in the well. Use your hands or a wooden spoon to work the dough. You should keep kneading the dough for at least 10 minutes until smooth and elastic. Then, cover the dough with a towel and let rest for 1 hour. Distribute the dough into 4 pieces. Roll out each piece to 1/4 inch thick with a rolling pin or a pasta machine, and cut into 3-inch squares, discarding the uneven edges. Place 2 teaspoons filling into the center of each square. Moisten the entire outer edge with water, bring the 4 corners together in the center and pinch tightly to seal, then pinch together the 4 straight edges to seal completely (take care with this step, sealing the dumplings thoroughly will insure that they will not become unsealed in the water and lose the filling). Repeat with remaining pasta and filling. Place the manti on a lightly floured baking sheet in a single layer.

Make the yogurt sauce: Drain the yogurt at room temperature through a very fine mesh strainer over a bowl for 30 minutes and discard the whey that remains. In a small wooden mixing bowl, add the yogurt and garlic together and keep it at room temperature until later.

To make the butter sauce; in a small skillet over moderate heat cook the butter until it is a very light brown, remove the skillet from the heat, and mix in the paprika, coarse salt to taste, and the hot red pepper sauce.

In a big kettle of boiling salted water, cook the manti, in batches, mixing to keep them from sticking together, about 7 minutes, or until the pressed together edges are al dente (they will take the longest to cook). Remove them when done with a long 1/4-handled sieve or a big slotted spoon and keep warm with a little of the warm cooking liquid. Serve the manti very hot in individual bowls, spoon some of the yogurt sauce over, drizzle with the butter sauce, and garnish with mint leaves. Pass the remaining yogurt sauce at the table.

Potatoes and Eggs (Patatesli Yumurta)

Sounds like American comfort food, but this has a unique Turkish flare. This is a great breakfast dish but it can also be eaten at any time of the day.

Ingredients
---

1 cup hash brown potatoes, frozen
2 tablespoons extra virgin olive oil
1 medium onion, sliced
1 garlic clove, sliced
2 eggs, beaten
salt
pepper
1/4 cup fresh parsley, fresh chopped
1 pinch red pepper, crushed (optional)

Preparation

In a big pan, saute the onions with the olive oil for 3-4 minutes. Next, add the hash browns, garlic, salt and pepper. Use a wooden spoon and stir constantly while cooking on medium heat for 8-10 minutes. Once the frying is done, add the beaten eggs and continue to mix. Sprinkle parsley and crushed pepper on top. You can also add yogurt on the side, or Cacik.

White Beans Plaki

Plaki dishes are famously Greek, such as Gigandes plaki, or "giant beans". South of Greece in the old Ottoman Empire, a variation known as white beans plaki exists; which also consists of specialty beans in a healthy vegetable stew.

Ingredients

1/4 cup olive oil
1 onion, chopped
2 cloves garlic, minced
1 big tomatoes, chopped (optional)
1 medium carrot, peeled and diced
1 medium potato, peeled and diced
1 stalk celery, thinly sliced
1 cup chicken stock
2 (15 ounce) cans butter beans, drained (or any other white bean)
2 tablespoons lemon juice
1 tablespoon fresh parsley
salt and pepper, to taste

Preparation

Prepare olive, onion, and garlic in a large-bottom saucepan on medium heat. Saute until lightly browned, and then add tomato, carrot, potato and celery. Mix and saute for another 3-4 minutes. Then, add the stock, simmer for 10 minutes. Add the lemon juice, beans, salt, and pepper, and continue simmering for 10 more minutes until the vegetables are tender and the stock is nearly gone. Remove from heat, mix parsley or other herbs and serve.

Yoğurtlu Şhish Kofte

This main course consists of skewered lamb kofte kebabs with a combination of yogurt and tomato sauces, creating a unique, flavorful dining experience.

Ingredients
500 g (1+ lbs) of lean ground lamb or beef
1 small onion, grated
1 egg
1 garlic clove, mashed with salt
2 day old slice of bread without the crust; soak into water and squeeze
1/2 bunch of parsley, finely chopped
1 tea spoon red pepper, powdered
1/2 tea spoon cumin
1/2 tea spoon crushed pepper
Salt
Pepper

Tomato Sauce:
1 cup crushed tomato, canned
1 table spoon extra virgin olive oil

Salt
Pepper

Yogurt Sauce:
1 cup plain Turkish yogurt, plain, room temperature
1-2 garlic cloves, smashed with salt

Garnish:
1 table spoon butter
Red pepper
Cayenne pepper

Preparation

4 pitas or Turkish flatbreads, cut into corners.

First create the kofte by mixing together the ground lamb, herbs, spices, and egg in a mixing bowl, Knead the ingredients together, and then begin rolling them into individual balls. Next, apply the kofte balls to the skewers. Starting from the top of each skewer, squeeze and flatten it so that it acquires a thin shape.

Preheat your barbecue or oven (grill). Place the skewers on the rack. Make sure to turn the skewers so that all sides of the meat cooks equally.

Cook the tomato sauce for a few minutes, put aside. Whisk the yogurt sauce ingredients, put aside.

Arrange the pita or flatbread on a serving dish, and place the kebabs over them, and then pour tomato and yogurt sauce all over. Melt the butter in a small pan and add in the pepper. When the butter starts bubbling, pour over the kebab, as well. Arrange with fresh chopped parsley on each end.

DESSERT

Turkish desserts are a unique gift to the world. You will find many of the standard desserts of the world in Turkey: custards, pastries, cakes, etc. However, you will quickly find that the Turkish style is always a bit different compared to what you're used to. From the inclusion of exotic spices, to the slow aging process that goes into baklava, foodies and travelers from around the world agree that Turkish desserts are not like anything else. Here are some of the most well-known that you can impress your friends by cooking.

Apricot Compote (Kayisi Kompostosu)

A sweet, fruity dessert served cold and could be brought on a picnic.

Ingredients

6 fresh apricots, peeled, pitted, sliced
1/3 cup sugar
2 cups water
1/2 teaspoon almond extract
1 package of almonds, roasted if you prefer

Preparation

Add sugar and water to a medium cooking pot, and reduce the heat to medium – low. Add the apricots and almond extract, and cook for 6 minutes or until sugar begins to caramelize slightly. Pour into a bowl and let it cool in the fridge. Serve with almonds.

Baklava

Arguably the most famous of all Turkish foods is baklava. An evolution of desserts from ancient Roman times, baklava is a sweet dish that had graced royal Ottoman courts for centuries. Today, dessert shops in Istanbul are filled with baklava and similar pastries to entice hungry window-shoppers.

Syrup:

2 cups sugar and 1 cup honey
1 1/2 cups water
2 tablespoons lemon juice
2 (3-inch) sticks cinnamon (optional)
4 to 6 whole cloves, or 1/2 teaspoon ground cardamom (optional)

Syrup

A Turkish Cookbook for Beginners

1 pound blanched almonds, pistachios, walnuts, or any combination, finely chopped or coarsely ground (about 4 cups)
1/4 cup sugar
1 to 2 teaspoons ground cinnamon
1/4 teaspoon ground cloves (optional)
About 1 cup (2 sticks) melted butter or vegetable oil

Pasta

1 pound (about 24 sheets) of phyllo (filo) dough. You can buy this at a specialty store or make it yourself. To make it yourself, you need a pasta machine so that it comes out as thin as you need it. I found a great recipe for authentic Mediterranean filo at the following link: http://greekfood.about.com/od/greekbreadspitas/r/phyllo.htm.

Preparation

First we must make the syrup. Mix the water, sugar, lemon juice, honey, cinnamon sticks (or cloves) on a low heat for 5 minutes, until the sugar starts to dissolve, while stirring the whole time. Stop stirring and turn up the heat to medium and continue cooking until the mixture becomes a bit syrupy, which will take about 5 minutes. At this point, discard the cinnamon sticks and cloves and let it cool.

Mix together all of the filling ingredients now.

Preheat the oven to 350 degrees. Grease a 12-by-9-inch or 13-by-9-inch baking pan.

Place a sheet of phyllo (as thin as you can find or make) in the prepared pan and lightly brush with butter. You will then add 7 more sheets. Spread with half of the filling you made, and then add 8 more sheets on top, brushing each with butter as you go. Use any torn sheets in the middle layer. Spread with the remaining nut mixture and end with a top layer of 8 more sheets, continuing to brush each with butter. Trim any overhanging edges.

Using a sharp knife, cut 6 equal lengthwise strips (about 1 3/4 inches wide) through the top layer of the pastry. Form diagonal cuts across the strips to form 1 1/2 inch-wide diamond shapes (four total).

Just before baking, lightly sprinkle the top of the pastry with cold water in order to keep the pastry from curling.. Bake for 20 minutes. Reduce the heat to 300 degrees and bake an additional 15 minutes until the surface looks golden brown / caramelized.

Now cut through the creases you created earlier, and drizzle the syrup slowly over the baklava. Then, allow it to cool for at least 4 hours. Authentic baklava is actually "aged", which means you will want to cover it and store it at room temperature for about one week. Keep extra syrup available to pour over the baklava during this process in case it starts to dry out / become crispy.

As for the "green stuff" commonly seen on baklava, these are ground pistachios. Try roasting a cup of pistachios, crushing them, and sprinkling on top.

İncir tatlı

A typical fig dessert you can find in the windows of Turkish cafes everywhere. Incir tatli may also include pastry fig dishes, as well. This is for the "gluten free" version without the pastry part.

Ingredients
250g (1/2 lb) dried Turkish figs. Prepare them by washing them and soaking them in hot water for about 15 minutes. Drain and cut off the stems
1 cup milk
1 cup 2% cream
1/2 cup sugar

Garnish:
1/4 cup walnuts, crumbled
Cinnamon, optional

Preparation

Cut the figs into bite size chunks, and then add the sugar, milk and cream into a big pot and mix at medium heat until all the sugar is dissolved. When the milk is warm, add the figs and cook until soft.

Serve warm or chilled with crumbled walnuts and cinnamon.

Muhallebi

Muhallebi is Turkish for "custard" and you'll find varieties of it at every diner in Istanbul. Small differences denote the ethnicities of where a particular custard originated from, with Lebanese muhallebi containing pistachios, for instance. This Turkish recipe calls for almonds.

Ingredients

1 liter of milk
2 cups water

¾ cup white rice flour
1½ teaspoons vanilla powder
¼ cup sugar
½ teaspoon rose water
½ teaspoon blossom water
½ cup ground almonds
Optional: Raisins, small bits of fruit

Preparation

In a bowl, mix together vanilla powder, rice flour, water, and a dash of the milk. Meanwhile, in a cooking pot, begin heating up the rest of the milk.

Wait until the milk is close to but not boiling. Now, pour it over the mixture, mixing thoroughly the whole time.

Return the mix to the cooking pot and now add the rose blossom water and sugar, as well. Bring to another near boil while stirring continuously.

Pour the mixture into small bowls, and garnish with the grated almonds or pistachio.

Semolina Halva

Halva is a traditional dessert that can be kept at room temperature. It literally means "sweet". Versions of the halva recipe can be found across the Mediterranean.

Ingredients

125 g butter
1 cup semolina
1/4 cup pine nuts OR pistachios
1 cup water
1 cup milk
1 1/2 cups sugar

Preparation

Melt the butter in a cooking pot on medium heat. After the butter has melted, add semolina and pine nuts, roasting these ingredients together until the pine nuts are a golden brown color. Then add water, milk and sugar, increasing the heat enough until a low boiling simmer is produced. Lower heat, stir occasionally, and wait until the water evaporates. Turn off heat, cover the lid on the pot and allow to cool to room temperature. Scrape contents into casserole dish.

And we've come to our conclusion.

I hope that this book has provided you with not only a basic understanding of how to perform Turkish cooking, but also the ability to master some of these recipes, which will allow you to create some truly exotic flavors that will BLOW AWAY people's minds the next time you're at a dinner party or picnic. Best wishes, and perhaps I'll see you in Istanbul.

About the Author

Chef Ayaz Babacan hails originally from Ezmir, a coastal city of Turkey. Born in 1973, he attended culinary school in the United States and returned to Turkey in 1999, and by 2005 he successfully opened and sold two restaurants specializing in basic, nuts and bolts Turkish food to introduce his regional flavors to travelers while providing great dining experiences for locals, as well. He currently lives in Istanbul with his wife and youngest of two sons.

Printed in Great Britain
by Amazon